DATE DUE			

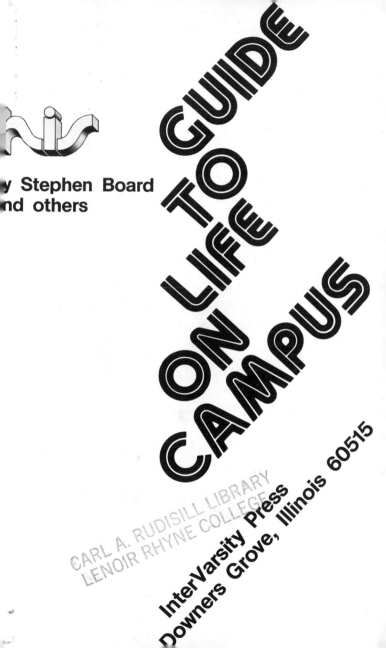

by **Stephen Board**
and others

GUIDE TO LIFE ON CAMPUS

InterVarsity Press
Downers Grove, Illinois 60515

Second printing
December 1973

© 1973 by Inter-Varsity Christian Fellowship
of the United States of America

Articles printed here originally appeared in
HIS magazine, published monthly October
through June, © 1961, 1963, 1966, 1969,
1970, 1971, 1972 by Inter-Varsity Christian
Fellowship.
To subscribe write HIS magazine, 5206 Main
Street, Downers Grove, Illinois 60515.

InterVarsity Press is the book publishing
division of Inter-Varsity Christian Fellowship.

ISBN 0-87784-355-4

Printed in the United States of America

CONTENTS

*Students can learn of Inter-Varsity's activities on the campus they expect to attend by writing the Chapter Secretary, IVCF, 233 Langdon, Madison, Wisconsin 53703. Canadian students should address IVCF, 745 Mount Pleasant Road, Toronto, Ontario M4S 2N5.

FOREWORD

The basis of this book is the simple conviction that the Christian can go off to the university and become a *stronger* Christian during those college years.

The modern secular university, itself, is no friend to God. Parents and older church people often have some reason to be anxious as they watch students move from high school to college, for the campus is a multi-media whirl of alternatives to a Christian life-style. But the alert believer, in fellowship with others who share his life in Christ, can find the resources not only for resisting temptation but also for winning fellow students to Christ.

In this brief guide some experienced campus leaders offer practical wisdom on life with God during the college years. Each chapter first appeared in HIS, the monthly magazine for university Christians. Most of the writers are associated with Inter-Varsity Christian Fellowship, a student movement active on many campuses of North America's colleges and universities.*

AGENDA FOR DISCIPLESHIP

1 All the dragons of the college years are obvious, but the choices in how to face them are not always so obvious. Here follows the HIS Guide to College Traumas.

If you take a poll of the crowds making their way to the campus counseling service you find their troubles organize themselves helpfully into a few categories. Knowing them, of course, doesn't solve all your problems but, as Samuel Johnson said about the prospect of being hanged, it helps to concentrate the mind. The lines of battle for the college student tend to cluster around (1) Vocational Dilemmas, (2) Inter-Personal Problems, (3) Sexual-Marital Problems, (4) Life-Style and (5) Intellectual Growth. It's in the nature of growing through ages 17-25 to work in these areas. The disciple of Christ is confronted with some choices.

Vocation Questions: What shall I major in? What am I interested in doing that is both fulfilling and marketable?

For the Christian student there are two additional ingredients in this question: the will of God and the ethical directives of his Word. You may expect some surprises in the future if God is guiding—you could be involved in several vocations. The will of God done every day adds up to the will of God for a lifetime. Likewise, Scripture does not call us to any conceivable vocation. We "test the spirits" here as anywhere else in life: money and success, as popularly understood, are not biblical criteria for choosing a major or a career. What's in it for God and the brother man?

Inter-Personal Problems: How should I relate to people I can't stand? How can I live with injustices, annoyances? How do I get people to like me? How can I get along with my parents?

Here the Great Divide is Philippians 2:21, "For everyone seeks his own and not the things that are Jesus Christ's." The standard non-Christian style of relationship is self-centered, a patchwork of angles and climbing techniques, so much so that the business world has gotten to the point of, literally, paying people to get along with each other.

The Christian alternative emerges from no longer knowing any man after the flesh (2 Corinthians 5), avoiding corrupt language that damages and selecting what edifies the other party (Ephesians 4). No easy task. It takes supernatural resources.

Sexual and Marital Issues: Whom shall I marry and how shall I relate to him/her before and after the wedding? How shall I modulate my feelings toward the opposite sex?

The issue here is not merely "keeping your hormones under control," as Archie Bunker thinks, but your whole slant toward sex and marriage. The secular choices narrow to two: the Glass-of-Water theory and the Woodstock Compromise. The Glass-of-Water approach says do whatever you feel like, your body ought to know what it needs. The Woodstock Compromise backs away from that pure hedonism and insists on the element of caring, if not love, in every sexual encounter. But the Christian has reservations about even this improved humanist version.

Scripture sees sexual intercourse as symbolic of unity and commitment—hence, as relevant only in a permanent context. It sees marriage as a team approach to the whole of life. This kind of vision puts the Christian student in tension with his culture and demands a disciplined strategy to see the Christian ideal developed in everyday experience.

Life-Style: What is essential and what dispensable? What costs too much, in time or

13

money, for me? Values expressed in priorities equal life-style.

If you step around this issue, somebody else will solve it for you. Every hour and every dollar are bid on by peers, profs, the crowd, home and the campus ethos. Nothing is easier than a life-style via crowd culture: all decisions tend to be based on immediate crowd considerations, money spent becomes the impulsive fulfillment of crowd values, priorities are set by an approximate average of your associations. Before you know it other people are living your life for you—and this can happen as easily in the critical youth culture as in the pressure of straight suburban life. The first casualty is always the thought life: solitude disappears, serious reflection evaporates.

It helps to think of your life as a production, a movie or play. Everyone has a producer who is arranging the set, imposing some direction, calling attention to the script, if there is a script. No one can handle this production by himself; everyone looks elsewhere for cues. It is our choice whether we will face a given day, or week, or year, under the direction of the Risen Christ or under the manipulation of circumstances and crowd. To many students, life seems meaningless because year after year goes by with no thought of who is the producer. The play comes out an irrational puzzle. "But you have not so learned Christ, if you heard him and were taught by him" (Ephesians 4:20, 21).

Intellectual Growth: I've registered for five courses. How are they connected? What does it matter? The semester costs $500; does that give me $500 worth of truth? Does Christianity hold up as true if I really sit down and study it out?

"I just take courses . . . none of them relate." A common student experience. The modern university is the world's greatest Fact Machine. It gives you the beads but nothing to string them on. It can tell you how to build a hospital or a bomb but not which of the two is the better. It perfects means but avoids ends.

If you begin this year a Christian, put it down from the start that commitment to Jesus is commitment to a great deal more. If God is the creator, the universe and the university have some genuine unity. It's like a long novel with many chapters, all related because of a single author. This means you can count on ordinary classwork to be a "spiritual" experience, research into the activity of God. See it that way and your study becomes a medium of worship, not a nuisance to get over with.

But along the way some conflict can be expected. Not everyone agrees that God is the Author of the Story of the Universe; some are passionately convinced he is not. Both cannot be right. Plan to do some hard thinking and serious reading.

For most people who enter college with faith in Christ, their four years on campus are the toughest test yet of the validity of the Christian way. Its truth is challenged, its influence is countered, weird arguments emerge to let slip the memory of Christ. Without getting hyper-defensive about the whole business, are you up to the challenge of this school year? Will it be a year as a disciple?

SPEND THE YEAR WITH GOD

 Why have you come to college? *"Well, because God sent me."* Why did he send you? *"I'm not exactly sure."*

Are you in this bind? Here are some possible solutions.

Remember how the Lord says in Isaiah 5 that he planted Israel like a vineyard in order to get fine grapes? It's the same today. He has planted you on your campus and expects a yield: righteous character and godly acts.

Practically, he wants you to be honest, attentive to his Word, diligent in study, concerned for others, a servant (like the good Samaritan) to the underprivileged—those who suffer from forces beyond their control.

In addition he is like an artisan working the clay. He wants to shape you to the image of his Son. Has he already sent a discouraging experience to toughen your faith, or a joy to remind you of his goodness?

Third, God's plan calls for you to be on this campus this year for use as an instrument in his hand to encourage other Christians on campus. Christians can be encouraged by your fellowship, supported by your prayers, comforted by your sympathy, strengthened by your association, taught by your example. Keep your eyes open for at least one other Christian to get together with to read God's Word and pray. Pray for him to become "rooted and built up in him and established in the faith" (Colossians 2:7).

Fourth, God will use you as a witness to those who haven't yet received Christ Jesus. This college is a mission field. Many are hungry for the Bread of Life—they may be students or faculty. (More professors than one might suppose are spiritually hungry.)

Here's a suggestion: Early in the semester, write on your prayer list the name of at least one student, maybe a roommate or classmate, who has no testimony for Jesus Christ. Pray for his salvation. Why not add the name of at least one of your professors to your prayer list? If you have a Christian professor, pray that he will grow in the Lord, and that the Holy Spirit may find him a usable instrument. And then pray for your profs who don't know Christ. Have you ever stopped to think that profound as their knowledge may be, if they aren't personally related to Christ they are in spiritual darkness?

Finally, you're at this school this year to serve as one of the dwelling places for God's Spirit at this institution. The faculty may pass legislation barring Bible study and prayer at this school but they cannot ban the Holy Spirit. Be his residence in your student body.

YOU CAN'T MAKE IT ALONE

 Of the hundreds of channel crossings I've made between Catalina Island and the California shore, this one was the most novel and crucial. A sudden illness at camp forced an emergency return not on my schedule.

The hospital nurse gave me a shot of morphine; the ambulance and crew assisted me to the waterfront; the doctor helped settle me in the small amphibian plane. Seat belts fastened, a small oxygen tank between my legs, oxygen flow checked, the doors closed and we were off.

Fifteen minutes later, with the oxygen gauge registering near empty, the plane touched down. In a few minutes it taxied to a waiting ambulance and a fresh supply of oxygen.

Fifty-four dollars later we were at the emergency entrance of the hospital. The men carried me in. I looked around to see the familiar faces of nurses well-known to me (this was to be my third extended visit in as many years) and exclaimed, "Boy, is it good to be home again."

The intensive care unit was the center of much concern and care with nurses, technicians and doctors straining day and night to save my life. I chafed and scolded (seeing doctors locked in their "deity syndrome" irritated me). Through it all, God graciously led me out of the deep, dark valley to the green hillsides of convalescence. But I never would have made it by myself.

So it is on campus. Though you're not usually carried there on a stretcher, you'll find yourself in a life-or-death struggle. You'll encounter forces bent on your destruction. You may be aware of some; others may be too subtle to recognize.

You're free to resist or accept the help other Christians offer in this tension. But like me you'll discover that you can't go it alone. The pressures of the classroom and college community alone will not cause your collapse, but your refusal to walk in conscious dependence upon God and in responsive contact with his children will. Perhaps as you wrestle with this problem your experience 21 will be something like the following:

those first days

On that first bewildering day of registration or classes you're met by a seasoned student familiar with the ropes who helps you with your first assignment!

You meet again at the Commons for lunch and find it a good idea. The feeling of aloneness in such a crowd is bad, and eating with others takes a bit of the edge off that emotion. It's good to know that some of the kids "brown bag" out in the quad. Not a bad idea.

You accept the suggestion to go to the bookstore with this newly acquired friend. The pointers on dollar savings on used books are a real help.

Stopping by at the Christian Fellowship booktable is something else. It is both frightening and sobering to see students with this kind of exposure. Their pitch is that this stop is as important as the one at the campus bookstore. Areas for study and reading covering a variety of subjects are outlined, and books you can borrow are listed.

The invitation to join others for Bible study and prayer—well, that's about enough. You'd think this was a Bible college! Oh yes, you find they meet periodically for lectures by off-campus big guns or Christian professors on campus. Sometimes they have training sessions on the basics of the Christian faith. On

occasion they just sing or goof around. Other

times they concentrate on presenting the option of Jesus Christ to their friends who don't know him.

Well, at first this is all right, but apprehension sets in as the days grow longer. Aren't they going a bit too far? And some of those students in the group—frankly, they leave a bit to be desired.

Then you say to yourself, "I'm going to go it alone." So you pull the bag over your head and try the incognito route. You studiously avoid "those people" and find your own way around without too much trouble.

a stranger

With the passing of the days, two things move in on you with distinct clarity. Different people from the group find you and make friendly overtures. One fellow comes on rather strong and indicates that you have to relate to others of like mind and faith or you won't make it. Somehow, birds of a feather must stick together.

At the same time you make another discovery. Though you are becoming quite accustomed to your scheduled routine, you find yourself increasingly a stranger in several classes. You frequently are alone in your philosophical and moral position. Positing the essentials of the Christian faith is looked upon with scorn or pity. Classroom discussion assumes sexual promiscuity to be the order of the day; as a matter of fact it is the accepted 23 practice in the dorm. Doing your own thing without any consideration for the authority of God is the in thing.

You're a stranger, out of step with most of those marching down the corridors of learning. You are gasping for air. You resist; you're trampled upon; you're pushed against the wall. You cry out, "Doesn't anyone care that I'm alone?"

Then you remember: "Lo, I am with you always . . . Where two or three are gathered in my name . . . Bear one another's burdens . . . Study to show yourself approved . . . Your Word is a lamp to my feet and a light to my path . . . Come unto me all you who are weary and heavy laden . . . Let the words of my mouth and the meditation of my heart be acceptable in your sight, O Lord my strength and my Redeemer."

Partly because he says to, partly because you need to, you cautiously start to accept the overtures of "those people." Sure, some are a bit odd, but you guess you are too.

You find you aren't alone in your feeling of isolation and frequent frustration. Together you share, pray and study. Together you reaffirm your trust in the Lord your God and his Word.

There are a few who turn you off. They are so holy! But you notice that others see through their facade and are helping them become "touchable."

They always seem to have time for you.

When you get bogged down with your studies, they come to your aid. They help you interpret the criticisms you receive on some of your papers. When you're discouraged, they slap you on the back; they humor you and listen to you.

You watch them challenge each other's positions. They disagree and agree; they're called on the carpet; they're helped along the way; they care for each other.

You watch them patiently relate to non-Christian friends. They proclaim, explain and listen. They get together with these friends again and again, instead of dropping them after a few weeks. They share their concern with fellow Christians. Their friends respect them.

After getting into some prayer meetings and seeing how they pray, you realize you were probably on one of their lists earlier in the year. That gets to you. Now you join them in praying for others and find that there are still many things you need to pray about for each other.

involvement

You've found that the Christian life is more than distributing cheap pulp newspapers or impersonally dispensing formulas for becoming a Christian. You've learned that fellow students are not prospects or problems but people, people with feelings and needs requiring more than slogans and slick answers. 25

You start pouring your life into others. You share your room, your credit card, your car and your bike. Your hands get dirty. You mix with colleagues of different political and religious persuasions, from different social and cultural strata.

In all of this you aren't alone. Sometimes you get yourself into corners and need fellow Christians to help bail you out—out of theology too deep for you, of physical needs greater than your resources, of various people-related experiences. You laugh and cry, cajole and support each other. Sometimes you are misunderstood. It is tough going, but great.

Oddly enough this also drives you to be alone for times of solitary study, reflection and communion with your Lord.

This, together with group confirmation, is of tremendous help in resisting the persistent pressure to conform to this world's view and be pressed into its mold.

Your progress chart, like mine in the hospital, shows fluctuations. You've had your highs and lows, mid-semester doldrums, doubts and discouragements. But to experience all of this with other Christians helps to filter out the insidious, contrary voices clamoring for your attention.

You know *that* you are, but you continue to ask and discover *who* you are. You keep learning *why* you are. In all of this you know that God is, but you perceive more and more who he is and what is involved in being his child through faith in Jesus Christ the Lord. You know in part now; someday by his grace you will have it all together.

Now that others have helped you "get your breath," and you are in good health, remember to reach out to fellow Christians who may be gasping. And be intently available to administer the first aid of friendship to those outside the faith.

You're part of the rescue team God wants to use in getting some other freshman to safety.

Like you, he'll never make it by himself.

RAT RACE

If you're in a rat race of activity, God can get you out of it. I saw him get Susan out of it.

She was a freshman when I first knew her, a student with a good mind and a pleasing way, attending college on an academic scholarship. She began to do a lot of challenging things. In the first place, Susan professed to be a Christian and wanted her friends to know Christ. She and Jean started a Bible study in the dorm. Then she worked with children in the town, another influence for Christ. Next came a community discussion group, and several other worthwhile things. At the same time many of Susan's hours were going into academic study. It was a busy, stimulating life.

But as the weeks went on, things didn't seem quite right. The Bible study group didn't get very far. Friends didn't seem too interested in Christ. In spite of her ability Susan found that studies were growing bigger than she was. A sizable problem developed over time. Activities seemed to be bumping into one another. Things begun were hard to finish. On and on it went—very unsatisfying, the parts not adding up to the amount she had figured on. Was this the Christian life?

Now, a year later, Susan is a different girl.

Did becoming a sophomore make the difference? Possibly, a little. Did she have a "scholarship chat" with the dean? I don't know.

I do know that Susan now has a serenity which speaks to me of Christ. I know that her roommate and another girl are thinking seriously about Christianity, and that the Bible study is catching fire. Other Christians on campus will tell you that Susan has been a great encouragement to them too (she meets regularly with some of them to pray). Her own time alone with God, placed strategically in the day, is a fruitful time now. Studies come second to it, but studies now seem to be the proper size (even though she studies more). I can see the beginning of a walk of faith. Susan has a look of peace about her.

One day while we were eating together I

asked her about the change. She said that this fall she had surrendered to Christ. Then, when his will was plain to her she followed him.

It was about December when Susan began to understand his will for her *time* on campus. She mentioned that she had only two and a half years more to be a missionary there, and she knew there weren't many missionaries among the hundreds of students. God was asking her to settle down to do a few things for him, she concluded—to do them well. He directed her to do three things along with her regular Quiet Time and studies. In her particular campus situation they made wonderful sense. (1) She should help lead the evangelistic Bible study, preparing thoroughly for it; (2) She should pray regularly with the other Christians; (3) She should have open spaces in her schedule for leisure with non-Christian friends. And that's the way she began to live: a few things prayed for, done in his power and with his character and peace. This is the life of faith.

Susan's interests are still varied, and she is learning in many areas of life. But the difference in her life is the result of giving everything to Christ, including her time. God's purpose for her is clear: she is to love him and do his will. And within his will for Susan are specific things, a few specific things that God wants her to do well. It is also his will, then, for her to let many other "worthwhile" things

go.

You can know God's will for you. The details may be different from what Susan found, but the principles will be the same: surrendering to him, asking him to be the manager of "your" time, doing only as much as you can adequately pray for and do in the power of his Spirit. Primarily it's a matter of using common sense about time for studies, meals, sleep and recreation.

"Unless the Lord builds the house, those who build it labor in vain . . . Apart from me you can do nothing."

KNOW GOD
THROUGH EVERYTHING ELSE

 "Knowledge is dangerous, suspect, destroys zeal. It's sure to drive you away from God." Sound familiar? I'm sure many students have heard this argument from certain well-meaning Christians. The charge it makes creates conflicts in the Christian who wants a solid education, so that it's important to examine the biblical attitude toward knowledge.

Scripture shows that knowledge, far from being intrinsically evil, is the gift of God. Psalm 94:10 speaks of God as "he who teaches man knowledge"; Colossians 2:3 states that in Christ "are hid all the treasures of wisdom and knowledge"; and Exodus 31:3

says that the Lord filled Bezaleel the son of Uri with "the Spirit of God, with ability and intelligence, with knowledge and all craftsmanship."

There's an important implication here: no man can know anything or do anything requiring particular ability unless God helps him. This principle is as true of cynical Voltaire as it is of reverent George Herbert; of the most godless composer as of Bach, who dedicated his work to the glory of God. Whether an artist uses his ability to glorify God or attempts to defy him, a well-executed work of art forms part of the glory of God's creation, since "every good endowment and every perfect gift is from above" (James 1:17).

So to study the arts is to study God's handiwork in human creation, just as to study science is to study his handiwork in the natural creation. The point is to worship not the artist, but the God who provides both artistic ability and individual insight. Similarly, from a religious standpoint, we master an academic field not to worship the human brain, nor the facts themselves, nor the scholars who have gone before, but rather to observe the way God planned things—in a sense, to think his thoughts after him.

For a Christian mind, therefore, no secular subject exists. Knowing that Christ is "before all things," and that "in him all things hold together" (Colossians 1:17), the Christian 33 freely pursues knowledge. He realizes that every area of knowledge revolves around Christ, the hub of the universe and therefore of the university. The more we learn about the universe, the more fully and intelligently we will be able to glorify the maker.

Unfortunately, many professors secularize their subjects by denying any connection with the mind of the maker. But this shouldn't stop the Christian from proceeding in the confidence that every facet of knowledge provides insight into the greatness of God's mind.

knowing god

At the same time, however, every Christian is ultimately responsible to pursue the knowledge of God. Paul was willing to cast all other accomplishments aside "because of the surpassing worth of knowing Christ Jesus" (Philippians 3:8). The importance of knowing God cannot be overstressed. The same Christians who fear knowledge say that the purpose of living is to win souls. "Learn a few simple techniques of soul-winning," these zealous people urge, "and don't waste any more time with knowledge." But a memorized formula for soul-winning can't make a witness out of a person who has not known God. (Who ever heard of calling a court witness who knew nothing about the case in question?) 1 John 1:3 provides the only real formula for witnessing, one which assumes individually acquired knowledge: "That which we have seen and heard we proclaim also to you."

This does not mean that you need a college education or formal education of any sort in order to witness. But the pursuit of knowledge in any area can contribute to a fuller knowledge of God. And the Christian bears witness to the knowledge that he possesses.

Pursuing the knowledge of God often seems a discouragingly abstract and nebulous quest. No one can set up a formula for knowing God because God deals with each of his children individually. But a few general principles may help.

knowledge is imperfect

First, full knowledge of God is impossible in this life. During these days of the absolutist-relativist controversy, 1 Corinthians 13:12 makes an important point: "Now we see in a mirror dimly, but then face to face. Now I know in part. . . ." It's very dangerous to forget that all human knowledge is partial and relative, limited by the mind and experiences of the individual. Those who forget the partial quality of their vision become rigid and arrogant, and dogmatically thrust their "infallible" knowledge of God's will on others. A Christian is an absolutist. He has an absolute frame of reference and knows that behind the glass is an absolutely perfect God who knows him perfectly. But he recognizes that he is limited to a partial and shadowy knowledge   35 of that God in this life.

Even though full knowledge is impossible, the Christian properly yearns after full knowledge. Ephesians 3:19 states the paradox in a prayer that Christians may "*know* the love of Christ which surpasses knowledge." At the end of his great career, Paul admitted that he still had not made it on his own, that he was still pressing "toward the goal" (Philippians 3:14). Browning caught the exhilaration of this philosophy in his famous lines from "Andrea del Sarto": "Ah, but a man's reach should exceed his grasp,/Or what's a heaven for?"

stillness

Second, the knowledge of God requires stillness: "Be still, and know that I am God" (Psalm 46:10). In context, the stillness involves trusting God's power rather than bows, spears and chariots. But the stillness might also involve the silencing of preconceived notions of God, and curbing activism. By rushing here and there, by choosing Martha's role over Mary's, we can be deflected from pursuing the knowledge of God.

Silencing the clamor of preconceived notions so that God can reveal his true personality often means unlearning false and damaging concepts of him. Browning deals with one such inglorious concept in his poem, "Caliban Upon Setebos." Caliban, an ignorant creature who is half-man, half-beast, sprawls in the cool mud thinking about the god his mother had taught him to fear, a vindictive god named Setebos:

He doth His worst in this our life.
Giving just respite lest we die through pain,
Saving last pain for worst—with which, an end.
Meanwhile, the best way to escape His ire
Is, not to seem too happy.

When a thunderstorm arises, Caliban is sure that a passing raven has told the god about his seditious prattling: so he bites through his upper lip in penance, and loudly proclaims how much he loves Setebos.

Like Caliban, certain Christians tremble before a Great Denier, a Cosmic Prosecuting Attorney whose chief joy lies in forcing them to sacrifice all the beauty and pleasure human life has to offer. Although they inevitably dislike such a concept, they loudly proclaim their love for him in their fear, lest he find some new way of tormenting them. Meanwhile, they build an effective barrier against a genuine revelation of God himself.

Or take the opposite concept, the still-widespread belief that God is obligated to bless the Christian who is completely dedicated to him, either with material blessings or with spiritual results in soul-winning and the like. Yet it was partly to refute this concept that the book of Job was written. It is easy to quote Job 37:23, "Touching the Almighty, we cannot find him out: he is excellent in power . . . he will not afflict." We forget that these words of Elihu are utterly repudiated as God speaks from the whirlwind: "Who is this that darkeneth counsel by words without knowledge?" God can and sometimes does afflict or permit affliction. He is under no obligation to explain why. He never told Job.

If we are to grow in knowledge of God, our spirits must be flexible and willing to accept whatever God chooses to show of himself, in whatever manner he chooses to make the revelation. "Be still, and know."

In his excellent study of Job entitled *Baffled to Fight Better,* Oswald Chambers describes how unsettling the experience of "silencing" can be:

> *Many a man has come to find the difference between his creed and God. At first a man imagines he has backslidden because he has lost belief in his beliefs, but later on he finds he has gained God, i.e., he has come across Reality. If Reality is not to be found in God, then God is not to be found anywhere. If God is only a creed or a statement of religious belief, then He is not real; but if God is, as the book of Job brings to light, One with whom a man gets into personal contact in other ways than by his intellect, then any man who touches the reality of things, touches God.*

behavior change

Finally, a genuine knowledge of God results in certain automatic changes of behavior. "He who says 'I know him' but disobeys his commandments is a liar, and the truth is not in him" (1 John 2:4). The chief commandment is to love, and love for others increases as we come to know God better.

Cardinal John Henry Newman comments on the results of pursuing knowledge in *The Idea of a University*. He says that liberal education viewed by itself, apart from God, can develop intellectual discipline and excellence, but only religious faith (the knowledge of God) can impart virtue:

> *Knowledge is one thing, virtue is another; good sense is not conscience, refinement is not humility, nor is largeness and justness of view faith. Philosophy, however enlightened, however profound, gives no command over the passions, no influential motives, no vivifying principles. Liberal Education makes not the Christian . . . but the gentleman.*

It is a good thing to be a gentleman, as Newman continues, but it is not the same thing as being a Christian, nor the same thing as knowing God.

The ideal is, of course, to be a Christian gentleman: cultured, intelligent, fully human, virtuous and dedicated. The knowledge of God imparts genuine virtues (like humility): "Now my eye sees thee; therefore I despise myself . . ." (Job 42:5, 6).

The ideal of the Christian gentleman is magnificently described in Isaiah 11:1-4, a passage which equates the spirit of knowledge with the Spirit of the Lord:

There shall come forth a shoot from the stump of Jesse, and a branch shall grow out of his roots. And the Spirit of the Lord shall rest upon him, the spirit of wisdom and understanding, the spirit of counsel and might, the spirit of knowledge and the fear of the Lord. And his delight shall be in the fear of the Lord. . . . But with righteousness he shall judge the poor. . . .

Modern Christianity stands in desperate need of wise and righteous leaders, people who have sought knowledge in every area, who have sought it in what Ephesians 1:17 calls "a spirit of wisdom and of revelation in the knowledge of him."

TRANSPLANTED

Probably your greatest period of change will occur between high school graduation and Christmas vacation your freshman year in college.

Horizons are expanding fast. Intellectually you're meeting great ideas, often communicated by men and women of impressive intellectual caliber. Socially you're moving among students with diverse backgrounds. In the arts your tastes are being cultivated and refined. And if your personality is maturing, your spiritual horizons will also expand.

As you're growing up in faith, you're probably facing new questions. Things are beginning to concern you now that didn't even 41 occur to you a few years ago. The religion prof drops a few words here and there that strike at the basis of your faith. At first you knew he was wrong. Now you may just be puzzled. After all he's a learned man, carefully trained, and obviously devoted to the important task of helping freshman think for themselves. Besides that, you like him. And he is able to explain some things you can't. Or can you? (At your stage of the game you may not be aware that another side of the picture hasn't been presented in class. There are answers that support the historic evangelical Christian faith and meet the demands of the most thoughtful.)

It is normal for you to have questions. It is wise for you to be unsatisfied until you've heard answers from intellectually able Christians who are confident in the trustworthiness of the Scriptures. Some help of this kind can come to you through discussions led by qualified men at regular Inter-Varsity meetings and conferences. Great help can come through the printed page too. (Especially recommended are: *The New Testament Documents: Are They Reliable?* by F. F. Bruce; *Runaway World* by Michael Green; and *Doubt* by Stephen Board. All are available from Inter-Varsity Press. The regular issues of HIS magazine deal with similar problems.)

And interestingly enough, a basic source of personal intellectual stability and discernment

is a regular devotional time. "The Christian

religion will hold up under close scrutiny, as will the Christian student, if he keeps revealing his life to Jesus Christ daily in his quiet time."

It is important in your freshman year to begin to integrate the Christian faith and the academic disciplines. A psych major I know said that he kept his learning in psychology separate from his "Christian life," probably thinking that Christianity wouldn't stand the test of psychological discovery. What a breadth of understanding could have been his, had he brought the two together with the help of books like *What, Then, Is Man?* (Concordia) and *Christ and the Modern Mind* (IVP). The bibliography *Encounter with Books* (IVP) will help you track down resources in Christian scholarship related to your courses.

friendship

Christianity is social; college is social. So Christianity has a unique opportunity to spread on campus. Wide doors of friendship continually open for sharing thoughts and interests. Non-Christian friends are all around and as you work together with them in the lab, and talk at lunch, strong ties will develop. In it all you can share Christ, indirectly through your attitudes and directly as you appropriately refer to him.

Apart from college, you'll probably never again have the same close associations that involve a natural give-and-take. Nor, generally speaking, will people ever be quite so ready to consider an outlook different from their own. It is in their freshman year particularly that students are open to see Christ in the day-to-day living of a Christian friend. And in seeing him, they begin to realize their own emptiness. As a freshman who places his trust in Christ, you have three more years on campus to live out the Good News among students who aren't acquainted with him, students who might not be reached any other way.

At one fairly small college six students became Christians, all of them freshmen. It happened as Christians became their friends and started dorm Bible studies. Then a number of freshmen were drawn into the larger weekly meetings. They saw something substantial there, something unselfish and kind. They noted in the discussions and in the dorm conversations that Jesus Christ was central, that Christianity is a Person who can be personally known. In time they gave their lives to him. All six, freshmen. All with new life. Don't miss the chance of living for Christ in such a way that your non-Christian friends will be drawn to him.

christian fellowship

The Christian friends you make can change your life. You don't *have* to seek them, of course. But you will please God if you do. And if you want to stay vital spiritually, you must. In the secular college situation you urgently need them.

In these other Christians on campus you will find treasure. Some of them will be different from you in culture, church affiliation, perhaps in ways of doing things—and even in appearance. At first these differences may loom large as obstacles to fellowship and you may have a yen for the old fellowship crowd at home. But if you persist in getting to know Christians at college, an amazing thing will occur. You will come to see Christ in them and they will become your most trusted friends. They will give you courage to follow God. By example and friendship, they will lead you on to a faith deeper than you have known. They will be one of God's most pleasant means of bringing you to greater maturity in Christ.

Not that you'll ignore non-Christians. But they'll have a different place in your life, even though some of them are more like you in social background. In the New Testament, Christian fellowship doesn't depend on cultural similarity; it is centered in Jesus Christ. If he lives in you and in your Christian friends, you'll have a oneness that secondary things can't dispel.

You need other Christians in college particularly because of the pressures that focus on you there. After being on campus about 24 hours, you probably began to sense a few of the things that bore down on you to grind 45 away at your obedience to Jesus Christ. Within a week you had experienced many of them. By Christmas you'll know them all. Some won't be new to you, but multiply by ten the pressures you felt in high school and you'll have an idea of college pressures. First is the constant academic demand. It takes a while to absorb the jump from high school to college. Then there's the unsettling pressure to conform socially, morally, religiously.

There's the endless round of extracurricular opportunities. Here you have to distinguish between contribution and growth on the one hand and on the other the amount of involvement that spells rat race. Many a Christian student has delved into just one too many activities, soon to find he's getting fuzzy spiritually and lacking keenness academically.

A dean in a well-known eastern college advises freshmen to move into just one activity in addition to studies. Studies, of course, are a prior claim and God is honored in them when you invest your best. In October, when courses are just beginning, you may feel you have time for more than one extracurricular. Don't be fooled. November brings a schedule of tests and papers that will take everything you have. Statistics of the United States Office of Education indicate that 40 per cent of the students who enter college fail to graduate; half of this 40 per cent leave college in their freshman year. The same dean I mentioned above says that "to prosper academically there is a practical single answer, an answer that is very simple and very difficult; you need to budget your time to best advantage." It means discipline. Have you learned to associate the word disciple with the word discipline?

As you participate in a Bible study with other Christians to consider God's principles of living and his standard of morality, you'll be strengthened in doing his will. This kind of support will be valuable to you in the midst of college pressures.

Certain aspects of the Inter-Varsity Christian Fellowship group may seem different from the high school group at home. You may discover, for instance, a change in the principle of leadership. Rather than a trained older person being the responsible leader, the students themselves take responsibility. The students have hammered out the group's goals for the year; students have planned how to reach these goals; students bring to the group appropriate people to lead the thinking in the weekly meetings: a gifted Bible teacher from the area for a series in a New Testament book, Christian lecturers who can focus on certain topics and answer some of your questions, perhaps a panel of students talking over their ideas and experiences. As time goes on, you can have a part in planning and in the panels. You'll see possibilities for new approaches and needed emphases, and as you give yourself to the group you can suggest these and 47 help carry them through.

In this connection it's helpful in the first weeks to learn as much as possible from the group, rather than try to assess its effectiveness. If you give yourself to group activities, you'll learn what makes it tick and your appreciation will grow unexpectedly. You may come to see, for instance, that some of the leaders of the group who are juniors and seniors have experienced two or three years of living for the Lord on that campus and their approaches may be more appropriate than they appear to you at this early moment in your college career.

This isn't to say that the IVCF group will be perfect. Far from it. It can't be. But if you withdraw from it because it isn't all it could be, the group will lose what you could offer by way of help. And you yourself will experience great loss. Christ's word to us to love one another isn't a bit of advice; it's a command. To demonstrate God's love for others we must spend time with them. To withdraw, then, is to disobey. To withdraw is to deny a primary New Testament teaching that Christians are interdependent in the same way as parts of a human body. To stay with the Christians and contribute to them is to please God, and as you do it he'll give you his love for them. Not a love that derives from similarity of background but rather a will to love. God had such a will toward us when we were totally unlike him, and gave his Son to meet our need.

What does fellowship among Christians do for the Kingdom of God? It moves it along. It nourishes Christians. It spells out the love of God to others.

Within the larger fellowship of weekly meetings and week-end conferences are opportunities for more personal fellowship. Ask God to give you one Christian friend of your own sex with whom you can meet regularly to talk and pray. This may be an upperclass student who's been along the path ahead of you. When you're with someone who's been having a meaningful Quiet Time, you'll become convinced that an effective daily devotional time is the key to enjoying God and living for him.

Of particular help to many students has been a unique Bible study guide that takes you carefully through basics for Christian students. Its title: *Grow Your Christian Life.* Many Inter-Varsity groups bring together each week those who are using it in their Quiet Time in order to discuss informally the leading ideas or questions. (Sample topic considered in this Guide: the place of intellect in personal evangelism.)

If the Christian fellowship group is vital, its members will major in helping others to know Christ. You may want to team up with another Christian or two from your dorm to invite an experienced person from the community or IVCF staff to lead an evangelistic discussion with your friends. As you continue in God's purposes with other Christians, he'll perform a wonderful work; he'll knit the Christians together in a way that no human organization could begin to do.

Christian fellowship is a gift of God to you because he loves you and knows how much you need it. It's a gift that can be easily damaged if you take it lightly ("Oh well, I'll get together with those kids sometime when nothing else is happening"), or if you're snobbish ("How can anyone have fellowship with people who have such corny attitudes?"), or if you're thoughtless with other Christians when you're with them ("I don't want to appear critical, but I think the way you guys have been approaching things is pretty bad; I have a better idea"). Be careful with this treasure, Christian fellowship.

What if there's no Christian group on your campus. Is everything a total loss? If you're in the college that God has selected for you, you can trust him to provide what you need. Ask him to lead you to another Christian, and when he does, plan to get together often at regular intervals. If no one shows up for a while, continue to trust God, knowing that he himself is a companion and friend who won't leave you. Try to keep in close correspondence with Christian friends at home and at other colleges.

An important off-campus help that God
may provide for you during college is worship

each Sunday in an evangelical church. This can be a significant means to strengthen you in faith, acquaint you with Christians in the community, and keep you in touch with life beyond campus. In one west coast community, Christian students were "adopted" by praying townspeople who invited them into their homes. And a new dimension was added to Christian life and witness on campus when community people prayed for students on the basis of personal acquaintance. You need the local church. Don't neglect it.

So now you're at the start of four years of college, a wonderful privilege, a trust from God. If Jesus Christ is the Lord of your life, these four years can be full, happy and valuable. If you'll love God and others for his sake, he can build into you a quality of discipleship that will make all the difference, now and in eternity.

THE ENLIGHTENED FRESHMAN

7 Mom said I should keep a journal, so here goes nothing. Me and one high school diploma—ready for the first semester of college. The folks seemed to have a hard time leaving me here this morning. They tried to look cheerful, but I think they were worried. I don't know about what, though. I'm just going to college and getting an education. There's no such thing as too much learning, is there?

The campus is sure a beautiful one. Green lawns and flagstone sidewalks wind in and out among granite buildings that must be at least fifty years old. And this afternoon I made it down to the science quadrangle. I'll be spending a lot of time there in the next four years. The architecture is more modern and sleek, sort of cold and formal. They say the equipment is the most up-to-date of any school in this state, and the profs are supposed to be tops.

september 8

Today we registered. It was a beautiful day, big warm yellow sun filtering down through just enough fluffy clouds to keep the blue from being monotonous. It's funny, though, the way most of the returning students walk around squinting. I'm amazed that they don't bump into things or people. They seem to know their way around, but how can they enjoy the beauty of their own campus with their eyes closed? I commented to a junior down the hall on how impressive the campus looked. But he just scowled and muttered, "That's OK, frosh, enjoy it while you can. You're only naive once."

My roommate came in today. Most of us frosh are from city high schools, but his folks are filthy rich, and he's just had three years at one of those swank prep schools. I offered to show him around campus to help him get oriented, but he wasn't interested. He said he couldn't be bothered with such childish things, but I could humor my own fancy if I wanted. Strange, but he's so much like the upperclassmen. He too keeps his eyes closed all day long.

september 12

First day of classes today. The most interesting by far was physics class. What a scene—there must have been three hundred of us in there when Prof. Scotus took his place at the front of the lecture hall. I've known about "Scotty," as the students call him, ever since I was a sophomore in high school. His picture was in all the papers for landing an international award in theoretical research. And they say that the textbooks he's written are known and used all over the U.S. and Europe. I guess he really must know his stuff.

I was way in the back, but I could have sworn he had his eyes closed just like everybody else. Instead of starting out with physics, he told us that since most of us came from small town backgrounds, he had better get us oriented to formal scientific thought. His comments went something like this:

"Most of you have grown up in rather sheltered environments, cut off from an atmosphere of scientific study and rigorous thinking. This has been fine for your early years, but now you are becoming adults. At the university we take very seriously our responsibility in preparing you for mature roles in our changing, technical society.

"When you were younger, your parents clothed you in diapers and booties, and proclaimed you well-dressed. You were well-dressed, too—for your age. But I dare say very few of you are wearing diapers today. [Everybody giggled.] As a matter of fact, if you were to see one of your classmates or professors strolling across the quad some fine morning in pink booties, diaper and ribbon-decked knitted bonnet, you would think him very poorly dressed indeed. [Burst of laughter]

"In the process of growing up, a person must change the types of clothes which he wears. Just so, we have found it necessary to change the ideas and concepts by which we live as we grow older. As youngsters, we are spoonfed certain ideas by our parents, and we accept them uncritically. But as we grow older, we learn to question and test them logically. Many of our ideas we find faulty, and discard. This does not mean that we were wrong in holding those ideas as children or that our parents were wrong in giving them to us, any more than they were wrong in giving us diapers. But the tragic thing is that some students reach college without ever discarding the concepts that served them in their youth. They come to our campus here still wearing their intellectual diapers! [Another burst of laughter]

"Let me give you an example. Yesterday was a pleasantly warm day out on the quad. As I strolled across to my office, one of the freshmen greeted me in passing and asked if I didn't think the Sun was beautiful today. I had to stifle a laugh. To think that a student could be admitted to a school this highly rated, and still believe that there is a Sun. I'd say he's long overdue for a change of diapers!" [Explosion of laughter, the bell rang, and we surged out.]

He's really got me thinking—and confused. What does he mean, still believe that there is a Sun? How could you *not* believe in a Sun? You feel its warmth, it makes the plants grow and anybody can see it. All they have to do is open their eyes. I'm determined to have a talk with my roommate about this.

september 14

Mel (that's my roommate) has been on my back for two days. When he found out that Prof. Scotus' ideas were bothering me, he mocked me out. "Don't tell me you still believe in the Sun myth?" he snapped. "I bet you think a fairy will bring you a quarter for the next tooth you lose. You're really in Never-Never Land, Junior. This school has sure got its work cut out with you!"

I've been talking with the other freshmen. Some of them say they never thought much about the Sun question before, but the prof makes sense. Besides, he must have studied it a lot, so they guess they'll go with him. Most of us are still confused. I think the only way to get to the bottom of this is to go talk to the prof myself.

september 20

Scotus was very understanding when I visited his office. He didn't try to laugh me down 57 like Mel did. And he took a real interest in my questions. He explained to me that men used to need a way to understand things like heat and the difference between night and day. So they began to tell stories about a great glowing ball of fire up in the sky. They used to squabble over their pet theories. Some said that the ball went around the earth. Others insisted that the earth went around the ball, spinning like a top. But in any case, when the ball of fire (they called it the "Sun") was on one side of the earth, that side had "day." The other side was "night."

But when men began to take science seriously, they realized that there was no need for a Sun to explain heat or night or day. Night and day are just other names for "sleeping time" and "waking time." When we sleep, that's night. When we're awake, that's day. We now know that the only distinction is a result of the way our bodies operate, so there's no need to invent some outside object, the Sun, to explain night and day.

Heat, the prof said, used to be explained as the result of this Sun. All heat either came directly from the Sun or was stored up by something on earth and released later. But now that we have developed more scientific instruments, we have determined that the center of our planet is very hot. Near the surface of the earth, high temperatures turn rock to putty so that it sometimes bursts through the crust. Even without this volcanic action, the hot core is continually radiating heat energy through the earth's shell. And it is this inner, geological heat, trapped by our atmosphere, that keeps the earth warm enough to sustain life. There is thus no need to postulate the existence of a Big Stove in the Sky.

He still hadn't answered my big question. So I asked it outright. "Why don't people just open their eyes and look? Can't they prove that the Sun exists just by looking at it?"

Scotty smiled sympathetically. The corners of his sealed lids flickered with jesting creases, and he leaned toward me. "Have you never had a dream?" he queried.

Of course I had, and I told him so. Then he explained, condescendingly, that ever since man first dreamed, he has known that he cannot trust his eyes. Men have dreams, visions, hallucinations and a myriad of other things that prove their eyes are not honest. So we can't trust our eyes, for they may deceive us. The only honest, scholarly thing to do is to close one's eyes. Then there is no danger of becoming confused between what one sees and what is false. A man is liberated from dependence on his eyes and free to use truly objective, sophisticated scientific instruments.

Scotty felt his way around the desk and walked me to the door. Most of my questions were gone, but I didn't feel at ease. Outside, the warm air was heavy with the aroma of burning leaves, and the breeze pressed my shirt against me and tickled my ears. And somewhere on the main drag in front of campus, a car blew its horn angrily.

october 18

Mel has been a lot more civil since I went to see Prof. Scotus. Last week we had quite a discussion in the dorm over the Sun question. The idea came up, from one of the other frosh, that a lot of things would be easier to explain if we just assumed that there was a Sun. Things like where heat comes from and why it gets cool at night. But Mel really put him down. A "simplistic obscurantist," he called him. "After all that science has proved to us mathematically and objectively, how could anyone be so naive as to accept that trivial a solution?" he snorted. "It's just not scholarly!" And that settled that question.

Mel has put a lot of time in on the Sun problem. He really has thought it out. I didn't like him at first, but it's hard to dislike a guy who is so concerned about being honest and fair with the facts. And I don't think he puts guys down just to put them down. He genuinely wants them to come to grips with the problems that are there.

He has a lighter side too. Once he mused to me, "Things would be fun if we could see—could *really* see, I mean, objectively. When I was still a kid and believed in the Sun myth, I used to be enthralled with colors, the beauty of flowers and the delicate balance of crystal snowflakes. And I thought that someday I might like to be a painter and capture the wonder I saw around me for others to enjoy. But then I learned that I would only be perpetuating a hallucination, recording a lie. And I had to be honest."

He had to be honest. I wonder—don't I have to be honest, too?

january 12

The holidays weren't much fun. Mom and Dad had gone to a lot of trouble to decorate the house, so that I could enjoy the vacation spirit. But you can't trust your eyes, so how do you enjoy what may very well not be there? There was a lot of hustle and bustle—visiting relatives, eating big suppers, going to parties. But the intellectual atmosphere was sort of empty. Whenever I asked a question about the "way we have always done things," all I could get would be a funny look or a discouraging comment. No one was curious about the way things really are. And the folks could not figure out why I spent so much time with my eyes closed.

There's a student on our floor who's new here this semester. He's a very naive guy—goes around talking about bright sunny afternoons and brilliant sunsets. But Mel and I will straighten him out before too long. Then he will become enlightened like the rest of us.

YOU'LL FIND
ME ON EVERY CAMPUS

 A few months ago, I uncovered a book review that I'd written as a student at U. of California. The subject was "On the Altering of Beliefs." I was almost 19 years old then.

"It is Saturday night," (I read). "I am in the reserved book room, where deep stillness is as refreshing as it is profound. I have been reading and enjoying Anatole France's *Penguin Island*. I wonder why. Two years ago I would have thrown the book away. . . .

"For as long as I can remember, God, religion, Jesus Christ and heaven have filled my mind and soul with vague, symbolic notions. I loved to defend them. . . . Then I came to the university. Tonight a college education seems to me nothing but a tearing down. English, psychology, geology, astronomy, philosophy and now even journalism are eager to show that Christianity is full of holes and fallacies. It seems that atheism is wisdom inside these portals.

"I no longer question the validity of their attack. Who am I to say they are not right? I see too that religion is but a remnant of superstition, that reverence is hypnotism. . . . It's all over now. When I sit in a church I feel I have gone back in history 500 years. Everything there is contrary to my reason, my senses. . . . My childhood images have been destroyed; I shall spend a lifetime shaping new ones."

reflection

Now forty years later, as editor of a Christian magazine, I think back to that lonesome little guy in the reserved book room whose yellowed theme I hold in my hand. He was a loser. He missed out. Campus evangelism passed him by, so that for another eleven years he remained outside of Christ. For three years he worked and hoped to be the editor of the *Daily Californian*. When it was awarded to someone else, his campus world came apart. He didn't know that God chastens those he loves in order to mold them into what he knows will be more usable instruments. He didn't even know that God loved 63 him. So he got drunk.

How do I, a Christian editor, get to myself, the disillusioned journalism student? How do I, a believer, get to myself, a lonely, unhappy young skeptic? If you can give me the answer to that one, you'll have unlocked the secret of campus evangelism. Things around school haven't changed all that much, and you'll find *me* today on every campus in America. Our name is Legion.

approaches

Here are some suggestions that might help to pull a few drowning students out of the waters of frustration and despair. *First,* the campus soul-winner has to be sure that he is securely anchored himself. If he is not encircled by a sense of peace and Christlike joy, if he is just a religious loser floating with the rest of the losers, he might as well save his breath. The surest proof of the resurrection of Christ is not the empty tomb, or the appearances of the risen Lord, but the change that came over the disciples; and the one irrefutable argument for Christ on campus is what he does for his followers in the student body.

Second, the man who would win his roommate to Christ has to stop worrying about him. This is God's business. Many times our prayers for our friends are little more than articulated worry-beads. If you want to pray, then pray a victorious prayer, and thank God for what he is about to do. Claim your friend in the name of Jesus Christ, and get on top of your prayer life.

Third, let's stop pretending to be model persons. Let's start some human relationships going. Such a relationship between Christian and non-Christian does not require sinful indulgence; it does require understanding and compassion. The ones we seek to bring to Christ are not objects of our strategy—they are friends whom Jesus loves. Let's remember that we have nothing to offer of our own— just Jesus, that's all. Anything else is a fringe benefit and subject to contamination. Therefore we can afford to be ourselves and not have to pretend we are plaster saints.

I had some real hang-ups in my thinking back in 1930. The campus evangelist dare not overlook honest intellectual difficulties or try to explain them away with a wisecrack. It is part of being a friend to give a non-Christian helpful reading material that will counter Julian Huxley, Bertrand Russell, Anatole France etc., to say nothing of Bultmann and the God-is-dead theologians. Inter-Varsity materials that are available need much wider campus circulation.

response

Biologically and psychologically the student is not a student at all; he is a person on the edge of adulthood, lonely, wistful, and not a little scared. If he could be convinced that the way out of his bind is to give his life to Christ, I don't believe you could hold him back. If he could be shown that Christian living is normal as God meant life to be normal; that it has a built-in shock absorber like nothing else on the market; that the gospel is realistic and provides an answer that works; and that life in Christ keeps on getting better the longer one lives in the Father's house—you've just bought 51 percent of his stock.

Students are people. They're open, receptive, and thoughtful as they will be at no other time in life. They want to believe in something and are deeply hurt by what they see around them. When their ideals of society collapse, they sometimes build little fantasy worlds of their own. That explains a lot of today's student unrest. Who will tell them that fantasy holds no more security than General Dynamics? Who will make clear to them that there is no security in this life; that security is found only in him who triumphed over this life on the cross? Who will tell them that with Christ they can find the raw materials for remaking society; that his love is the one sure magnet to bring men together?

I wish I could go back to that reserved book room in Cal's Coe Library and talk to that fellow sitting there. But then, he is saved now; the Lord has him. What about all the others who are despondently thinking, "A college education seems to me nothing but a tearing down"? They are very lonely. Who is reaching them?

DEATH OF A ROOMMATE

Today we buried the girl who had been my college roommate years ago.

Yesterday I received a call from her mother and spoke with surprised pleasure—almost too gaily—until I realized that something had happened.

She said, "We've come back from California to bury our Kathryn in Michigan. Paul and their children are here with me." I hadn't heard of her death till then.

Kathryn was dead. She shouldn't have died now. She was too young. Her children needed her; her husband loved her. Nevertheless, Kathryn was dead.

It was as if I'd died. We'd known we would

die when we were older, but not now. We weren't very afraid of death, for life was good and sweet and fun, and now suddenly we weren't the invincible ones. We, the golden girls, the life of the party, the idealistic world-changers . . . it couldn't happen to us. But one of us had died. Suddenly I felt vulnerable.

I thought back over our college years and the silly things we'd done. We'd been roommates three out of our four years at Michigan State, both of us journalism majors. We took a year of Shakespeare together from a funny little professor who sat crosslegged on his desk and dramatized each character for us. We went for walks and talked about life.

Ours was the party-room in the corridor because our mothers sent the best "care" packages.

One Halloween we dressed up and attached ourselves to a group of trick-or-treaters and later sat on the curb in front of our dorm eating the goodies we'd collected. We went camping, visited each other's families, and laughed a good deal. I still have the telegram she sent when she heard of my engagement.

She was my bridesmaid; I was hers. We rejoiced with each other.

But I have more memories than this. We'd often talked together about God and how you could know him. We read the Bible together. One day she came into our room, all glowy and radiant the way a Swedish girl can be, and said, "I've met him." And since men are often the topic of dorm conversation, I asked without much enthusiasm, "Which man is it?"

She said, "The One who lives upstairs!"

Not too orthodox a way of announcing that she'd become a Christian.

The last time I visited her in her own home with her own family (a husband and three children who were awesomely like their happy parents), the Bible I had given her at the time of her conversion was on the nightstand by her bed. I opened it and read what I'd written on the flyleaf, and all the emotion of our becoming sisters in Christ came back to me.

And so I stood by Kathryn's grave today and wept. She had so much to live for, I thought, though more to die for. My tears were partly out of wonder—that God would put me in a certain hall in a certain dorm so I could be Kathryn's roommate, and she could hear about God's Son and become one of his. I was profoundly grateful that God had given her to me as my responsibility.

I wept for her mother because Kathryn was her only daughter. I wept for her children who needed her. I wept for her husband. And I wept for me. I wished I had done more. Life suddenly seemed so short.

Then I thought of you. What about your roommate?

BEFORE YOU PASS IT ON

Many people either don't get started in witnessing or don't get anywhere because they have the wrong mental attitudes.

Scripture says that our attitude is crucial in everything we do: "Be transformed by the renewing of your mind" (Romans 12:2). Our thoughts and attitudes determine our actions.

What attitudes should we have about witnessing?

First, we must be convinced that being a Christian is the greatest thing in the world. Once we're persuaded of that, we'll know that

the greatest favor we can do anyone is to introduce him to Jesus Christ. We need genuine enthusiasm about our personal relationship with Jesus Christ. If we don't have this attitude witnessing will be a constant drag—something we have to do, not something we want to do.

How do we get this attitude? It begins with total commitment to Jesus Christ. A half-committed Christian (if there is such a thing) can't help being unhappy. He's not sold out to anything. But the Christian who can honestly say with Paul, "To me to live is Christ," can have the same joy Paul had. It also comes with appreciating what Christ has given us. Too many of us, particularly if we've been raised in a Christian environment, have taken what we have as Christians for granted. Sometimes we feel cheated. We think non-Christians are having a ball, and secretly envy them.

We Christians need to ask ourselves, Where would I be if Christ had never entered my life? Think about it and you may find yourself surprisingly thankful. Ask yourself, "What does Christ mean to me today?" Don't ask what he is supposed to mean, but what he actually does mean. Does he give any sense of purpose? Is there any peace from knowing him? Do you sense any power in your life which is not your own? You may be surprised to realize all the things for which you haven't been thankful recently.

Think of some non-Christians you know

who have none of these and are giving their whole lives to things that end with the grave. If you don't know anyone like this, make a deliberate attempt to get to know some non-Christians on your campus. Many students are very open about their despair and aimlessness in life. Popular music and the drama frequently state this in eloquent terms. You can't help but be enthusiastic when you know you have the answer. Your enthusiasm will be even greater when you see someone become a Christian and pass from death to life.

motivation

A second important attitude will grow out of the first. We witness out of love for Christ and others, not to accumulate spiritual brownie points and advance our own status as Christians. Loving non-Christians means that we desire their best. We don't swoon over them sentimentally. We show we love Christ when we obey him (John 14:21), and one of his clearest commands is that we share the faith (Matthew 28:19, 20).

If we are convinced we're doing the other person a favor by witnessing to him, we won't be threatened if he doesn't respond. We'll be saved from the begging which often demeans the gospel. He'll realize we're not using him to advance ourselves, which he would resent, but genuinely want to share the most wonderful thing we've found in life. He's the loser if he turns it down.

A third attitude is realizing that God is the evangelist and we are his instruments. Even though we are God's only mouth and feet, the whole thing does not depend on us. The Holy Spirit creates spiritual interest. We can't create it, we can only discover it. God the Holy Spirit converts people. All we can do is issue the invitation. This realization will deliver us from fear. No one is beyond God's power. If a person understands and then rejects the gospel, they're refusing God—not us. This also saves us from pride. We may have the privilege of being the last link in the chain bringing a person to Christ, yet it's no credit to us because God gave the increase (1 Corinthians 3:6). We don't measure our spirituality by how many scalps we have. At the same time, we are alert to issue the invitation at every possible opportunity.

imperfect messengers

If God is the evangelist and we are his instruments, perfection is not required to witness. God even used Balaam's ass to convey a message when he had to. If we desire to please the Lord and try to live a consistent life, we must not allow the enemy to seal our lips by overwhelming us with an awareness of our failures. We don't invite people to become Christians because we're perfect, but because Jesus Christ is perfect. If we make ourselves hypocrites, no one will listen. If we show that we're sinners saved by grace, other sinners will be attracted.

Finally, we must believe that people are interested and will respond to quiet confidence. Most of us assume people aren't interested and almost apologize for bringing up the subject. If we don't apologize, we're generally so nervous that the other person becomes nervous too.

We must learn to relax. Try explaining the gospel to a friend as a beginning. You might even practice talking as you would to a non-Christian. Stand in front of a mirror and watch yourself. Getting used to hearing your own voice can help you relax. Then take the plunge. Nothing will persuade you people are interested until you are led by the Spirit to someone who is.

SAY WHY YOU BELIEVE

 Apologetics, the art of intellectually defending Christianity, is largely ignored in our day. Today most Christians emphasize the personal, emotional, gut-level Christianity that excludes intellectual matters. Unfortunately, this complete reliance on emotion is a shaky foundation for faith. In *The World's Last Night,* C. S. Lewis wrote that feelings cannot be our sole spiritual diet because it's physically and psychologically impossible to maintain a fixed emotional state. This is behind Jesus' command for a complete, balanced faith: "You shall love the Lord your God with all your heart [emotion], and with all your soul [commit-

ment], and with all your mind [intellect]"
(Matthew 22:37).

In a college environment, unbelievers may
well call upon the Christian student to fulfill
Peter's charge to "be prepared to make a defense to any one who calls you to account for
the hope that is in you" (1 Peter 3:15). A
strong case for apologetics can be made from
this one verse. The word used for "defense"
(*apologia* in Greek) is a legal term which
means the presentation of evidence to support
your position.

Every Christian has a duty to represent
Christ as well as he possibly can. Apologetics,
which provides the tools for this task, has
three categories.

First, we need to define precisely what the
Christian gospel *is*. Often the unbeliever rejects a caricature or perversion of Christianity,
not true Christianity. Knowing the content of
faith can clear away the deadwood and allow
important issues to surface. We need a mental
list of priorities so that we do not wage intellectual warfare over secondary issues while
letting more vital matters slip by unnoticed.
Jesus' interaction with the Samaritan woman
(John 4) should be our model here. He guided
her question about where she should worship
back to the more important issue of his own
Messiahship.

Second, we must engage in the negative
task of showing the weaknesses, difficulties
76   and contradictions in the non-Christian posi-

tions we encounter. This broad category includes at least three subdivisions. (1) Philosophical apologetics demonstrates the weaknesses of prevailing non-Christian philosophies (such as logical positivism, Marxism, existentialism, etc.). (2) Religious apologetics deals with the shortcomings of alternative religions (Hinduism, Zen Buddhism or modern cults). And (3) cultural apologetics seeks to show that the concepts underlying secular, twentieth-century culture, when extended to their logical conclusions, add up to zero.

The falsity of a non-Christian system does not automatically make the Christian position true. The apologist's third role is to provide positive evidence for the truth of Christianity. In the past, this evidence has come primarily from prophecy and miracles. Although prophecy has fallen into disuse, I am struck by the continuing truth of Pascal's statement, "Under the Christian religion, I find actual prophecy, and I find it in no other." Throughout the Old Testament, a prophet was evaluated by whether or not his prophecies came true. If they didn't, he was to be rejected (see Deuteronomy 13 and 18). In the New Testament too the effort is made, especially in Matthew's Gospel, to validate Jesus' authority by showing that Old Testament prophecies were fulfilled in him. That argument is still valid today.

The Christian's strongest evidence is the miraculous. Jesus and the apostles emphasized 77 this. Jesus said that all his claims to deity and Messiahship hung on the miracle of the resurrection (Matthew 12:39, 40). And the apostles also saw this event as central to their message (1 Corinthians 15:3-8). By marshalling the historical evidence on behalf of Christ's life, specifically the resurrection, the Christian can build a powerful case for the truth of the gospel.

To those two positive proofs, I would add what Francis Schaeffer calls the "final apologetic"—the changed life-style of the Christian. A missionary I know used to say, "Your lives are the only gospel some people will ever read: What do they see?" The apologetic of changed lives is both the easiest and the hardest to present—easiest because it requires no mastering of intellectual material, and hardest because it requires a daily surrender of life to God.

By sheer volume, the variety of apologetic methods outlined above may discourage potential apologists. Students have far more pressing demands on their time than reading scores of books on apologetics. I can sympathize with this problem. When intellectual difficulties with my faith bothered me, reading apologetic works was so time-consuming that it contributed to a dismal grade-point average.

To counteract this problem, I propose a mini-library of key paperbacks for apologetics. If they are read and kept handy for reference, they will supply a wealth of information on most apologetic issues that you are likely to encounter. The entire collection can be purchased for under $20.00, and should find a place on every educated Christian's bookshelf.

apologetic mini-library

(1) Gordon Lewis, *Decide For Yourself* (InterVarsity Press, $2.25). The author uses inductive studies from relevant Scripture passages to help the reader build a fully biblical theology.

(2) Colin Brown, *Philosophy and the Christian Faith* (InterVarsity Press, $2.50). Brown's work is historical as well as apologetic. Though brief, it contains many footnotes and a full bibliography to guide further research in specific areas.

(3) J. N. D. Anderson, *Christianity and Comparative Religion* (InterVarsity Press, $1.95). By showing the uniqueness in Christian concepts of God, revelation, salvation and ethics, Anderson provides a strong answer for those who claim that all religions are "saying the same thing in different ways."

(4) and (5) Francis Schaeffer, *Escape from Reason* and *The God Who Is There* (InterVarsity Press, $1.25 & $2.50). Francis Schaeffer is the best-known cultural apologist writing today. His nearly prophetic works show the bankruptcy of contemporary values and how Christianity can fill the resulting spiritual vacuum.

(6) Paul Little, *Know Why You Believe* (InterVarsity Press, $1.25). Little draws upon his wide experience in evangelism at colleges and universities to give chapter-length treatments of the most commonly met objections to Christianity.

(7) John W. Montgomery, *History and Christianity* (InterVarsity Press, $1.25). Montgomery collects a wealth of historical evidence on behalf of Jesus' resurrection and explores its relevance to apologetics and theology.

(8) F. F. Bruce, *The New Testament Documents: Are They Reliable?* (InterVarsity Press, $1.50). Dr. Bruce is one of the finest New Testament scholars alive today. In this work he surveys the evidence of archeology, secular, first-century historians and manuscript transmission to conclude that the New Testament documents, as we have them, are the most reliable historical records of classical antiquity.

(9) C. S. Lewis, *Miracles: A Preliminary Study* (Macmillan, $1.25). One of the most bothersome elements of Christianity for modern man is its inseparable connection with miracles. In his most philosophical work, C. S. Lewis presents a convincing case for accepting New Testament miracles.

A LONG NIGHT'S JOURNEY INTO DAY

Artists and writers are shouting at us to pay attention and face the cultural crisis. These men, equipped with radar to penetrate the smog of our spiritual environment, focus on one theme insistently: Human life has lost its wholeness and is falling apart.

On the whole, evangelical Christians are not listening, and the penalty for our isolationism is irrelevance—We aren't aware of the forms the root problems are taking. Killinger is right in saying, "When the church fails to listen to contemporary art, it usually misses the temper and mood of humanity and loses its opportunity to deal with the needs of man at the point where it might most readily have entered into them."

The horrible result is that the people who see the problems don't know the answers, while those who do know the answers, evangelical Christians, have hidden them effectively behind barricades of ignorance. Equally awful effects are visible within the church. We Christians, cut off from the world in which we were called to witness, have become preoccupied with our own in-group concerns and fail to speak about God's redeeming love to the culture around us. And because we do not care to understand the questions of the culture, we become vulnerable to these very problems themselves. The church is secularized in its sleep.

It is our responsibility to understand non-Christians. "As the Father sent me, even so I send you." Christ renounced the insignia of his divinity and learned to live in a strange milieu to save us. As his disciples, we must learn to die a little for others and take their burdens on our shoulders.

christians and culture

Taking time to understand our culture, however, is not a distasteful duty required for effective evangelism. Rich personal rewards accrue in the form of spiritual and mental growth. Henry Zylstra once remarked, "There is more of you, after reading Hardy, to be

Christian with than there was before you read him; and there is also more conviction that you want to be." He makes an exciting point. Culturally barren Christians are often small, ugly people. Their lives can be so unlovely, so incomplete, and so unattractive that the gospel they profess is dishonored. Beauty is no enemy of truth, nor is Christ the antithesis of culture. Cultivating our cultural potential is related to our spiritual maturity. When our mental powers are exercised and expanded, there is more of us to serve Jesus Christ! The American church must not allow itself to be caught up in the incredible barrenness of the secular TV culture. Its resources in Christ are so much richer that that. Therefore, the Christian owes it to his Lord to be a deep and sensitive person. This means entering into the significant experience of others.

Jesus Christ proved that it was possible to penetrate sinful society without assimilating its values. One need no more become bad by looking at badness than become triangular by looking at triangles!

Yet understanding our culture is not without its risks, of course. Christian teaching against "worldliness" from Augustine on has not been without some point. In the process of understanding the world, redeemed souls can be adversely affected by exposure to a steady diet of savagery and sordid sexuality. Modern films certainly inform us what life without God is like, but we cannot afford to be complacent about the cost of such information in our own lives. We have to wear two hats: Besides being analysts of the culture, we need to be something of the concerned prophet as well. We can't calmly uncover the nature and causes of our Sodom-like national spirit without at the same time shuddering at the imminent judgment of God. But the Spirit of God will keep us to the end. In his strength we can invade worldly strongholds and challenge Satan for possession.

a cultural apologetic

What I am recommending is the development of a convincing cultural apologetic.

Such an approach focuses upon the dilemmas of man as he himself expresses them. It points beyond them to the Christ who says, "Come to me, all who labor and are heavy laden, and I will give you rest." The cultural media supply a natural point of entry into the inner life of modern man. They reveal sensitive points of contact for the good news. The reason for this grows from the relationship between religion and culture. "Culture" is the expression of what lies in the heart of man. It is a "religious" response to his existence in that it tells us what his ultimate concern is, what his vision of reality is, and what he worships. A novel or play may not teach a point overtly, but it certainly has a premise. It expresses something about the situation of the artist and presupposes a religious commitment of some sort. Cultural apologetics is the art of penetrating down to the religious roots of cultural expressions. It probes the deeply religious questions which are posed from man's side in literature and art, and correlates them with the answers of the Christian faith.

Modern culture eloquently portrays life's emptiness without God, and its testimony is in a sense pre-evangelistic: It shatters human complacency and opens a person up to the gospel. Even the most anti-Christian novels are in one respect "religious." Behind the secular facade lie profound, unresolved questions which only Christ can ultimately deal with.

Modern literature is a vast repository of expressions of human need and spiritual insights. We must recognize this deposit and implement its possibilities in our apologetic.

The aim of cultural apologetics is relatively modest. It seeks to display the gospel against the dark backdrop of the contemporary intellectual climate, and to explain how it is possible to live a redeemed life on the basis of the Christian faith. In application, therefore, it needs to be bolstered by historical evidences in order to show that the gospel is factually true as well as existentially relevant. The appeal to "coherence" always demands factual verification as a safety precaution, since it is always possible by wishful thinking to create an imaginary paradise. In the Christian faith we have a historically-structured message, 85 open to investigation and confirmation, which can direct man today out of darkness into light.

It is our responsibility to understand non-Christians and relate the gospel to the questions they pose.

HOW TO
TAKE HOLD OF THE BIBLE

Have you ever asked yourself, "Why doesn't the Bible find its way into my life more frequently?" I have. We hear other Christians speaking about what the Scriptures mean to them, but perhaps it just isn't our experience. With a little bit of work, we can correct this.

How can we apply Scripture to our lives? Learning involves three steps. First we *observe* and try to see what the facts are; next we *interpret,* trying to make some kind of order out of the facts; and finally, we *apply* by finding a course of action.

Why has God given us his Word? Because it

is his basic tool to conform us to the image of Jesus Christ. All Bible study should lead us to the question, "What does God want me to *do* about the truth he has shown me?" I don't believe we really learn anything until we are implicated by some course of action that involves us in the truth. In that involvement (prompted by the Holy Spirit) God teaches us and changes us to become like his Son.

a plan

Let me share a plan that helps me to begin this process. Each week I pray that God will take one passage out of Scripture and make it real to my own life. During the week as I am reading according to some program, I analyze each day's passage by putting it into my own words. My goal is to get it into terms common today. In the course of the week one passage will particularly impress me, and on that passage only, I use an A-B-C approach. I *A*nalyze the portion as I described it above. Then I choose the *B*est verse, and usually memorize it. After this I usually make a *C*ontract. I find that Scripture breaks down into three main areas: commands to obey, promises to claim, principles to practice. My contract is related to one of these. I get a little squeamish at this point, because I know it is getting personal and I might have to do something.

The problem becomes one of leaving the general and coming to the specific. We often shoot at nothing—and hit it every time—in our

88

Bible study application. I usually ask myself a couple of questions. Where did I miss this in my life? Where can I practice or put this into effect in my life? Nail your course of action down. Make it so specific that you can't get out from under it. If God spoke to you about loving the people on your dorm floor, don't pray, "Lord, help me to love everyone on my dorm floor." Say, "Lord, remind me to pick up my clothes because my roommate is a meticulous person and my sloppiness bugs him." Or, "Lord, remind me to turn down the stereo when my roommate is studying because he can't concentrate," or, "Lord, remind me to turn the lights off at a reasonable hour when my roommate is trying to sleep." When you get this specific you are involved. We should not say, "I should," "I ought," "I must," etc., but "by your grace I will . . ."

Find someone who can share applications with you so that you can be more objective and also get help from a friend with your problem. Also, write your applications down so that you will have them for future reference. At the rate of making one contract a week, I find that I can't work on more than three contracts at a time or it becomes frustrating. So I periodically cross off some contracts as I add others. God can bring one I've crossed off to my attention again when that is necessary. Often I find that God will repeat the same application for several weeks with slight variations.

some examples

Here is a personal illustration to show how I do this in my life. A lady in California is a close friend of mine. After seminary we corresponded fairly regularly. Once she wrote me about an elderly woman in Indiana who was having a hard time making ends meet. She needed some help because she had no contact with relatives or churches. I wasn't scheduled to visit her town for quite a while, so I wrote a letter to the president of the local Inter-Varsity chapter asking him to look into the matter. Immediately I forgot it.

A month went by and no letter came from my California friend. The second month a letter came. It started out like this: "My Dear Precious Brother . . ." This woman is a real exhorter, and I knew something was coming. "I want to stir you up about a common sin of young preachers and Christian workers today . . . that is the sin of NEGLECT!" (She took one whole line across the page to write this last word.) My first reaction was, "My dear woman, if you only knew how much work I have to leave undone because I simply don't have the time to do it . . ." Since God had used this woman to speak to me many times before, however, something said I had better calm down before doing or saying anything.

The next morning I came across Proverbs 25:12, "Like a gold ring or an ornament of gold is a wise reprover to a listening ear." Ouch! I was writing an application that morning and immediately started to generalize. I told God that I was thankful that he had shown me this truth. I said I would try to do better in the future. God reminded me that I already knew I was to do better. The question was, What was I going to *do* about it. I could find no peace until I made a long distance telephone call and found out what had happened to the woman. In this case she had been taken care of. I also had to sit down and write a letter to my friend saying, "You are right, I am guilty of the sin of neglect." I memorized that verse in the hope that it would deter me from practicing the sin of neglect the next time.

I don't know what your application will be. You may need to make an apology. You may need to write a letter. Maybe you should memorize the verse or passage and review it every day for two weeks. Possibly you could pray about the area every day for two weeks. God will tell you what he wants you to do, but don't just stop with the truth itself. Go on to that course of action which will drive the truth into your life. In that way the Word of God will start to mold your life to the likeness of Jesus Christ.

WHEN THE PROF DISAGREES

What should a Christian do when his faith is criticized in the classroom by a professor? Should he challenge the professor in class or quietly endure the assault? This question gnawed at me as an undergraduate. At times I remained silent but then condemned myself for being such a coward that I would not defend my Lord. At other times I did speak up but then felt like a jerk because I had said the wrong thing and feared that I had discredited the gospel.

There are no easy answers to this question. But my perspective has changed now that I have spent some time on the other side of the lectern and have a better idea of what makes professors tick.

An attack upon the Christian faith is not the same as an attack upon our politics or our theory of aesthetics. It must be seen as one battle in a spiritual warfare and the Christian must be armed with the spiritual weapons necessary for this conflict (Ephesians 6:10-18). The Christian should respond with the mind of Christ. This response must be marked both by love and by a concern for truth. Love without truth is sentimentalism; truth without love is Pharisaism.

It is short-sighted to view our professor as a symbol of the ungodly university world. People were not symbols to Jesus; they were unique individuals in need of his love and concern. What is it that motivates your particular professor to attack Christianity? There is a sense in which the answer is simple: Satan. But that provides us with little practical help. Is your prof's antagonism motivated by ignorance concerning the nature of biblical Christianity or is it an emotional hang-up? Is he the type of person who enjoys attacking and degrading all of the significant objects in the world or is he consciously rebelling against the gospel? It is impossible to answer these questions until you begin to view the professor as a person.

As an undergraduate I discovered that some

of the most outspoken critics of Christianity

had come from Christian families and knew what they were rejecting. Others had never encountered genuine New Testament Christians and were speaking out of ignorance. In the latter case a number of these men changed their entire attitude toward Christianity as a result of meeting Christian students who possessed a warm faith and who viewed them as persons. Some became Christians.

The first thing to do in the presence of criticism of Christianity is to pray for God's guidance and perspective. Then discuss the matter with other Christian students and with Christian faculty who may be on the scene. Beware of an impulsive, individualistic response on your part that can very easily become an ego trip. We need the balance and the support of the Christian community during these times of stress.

the personal touch

The life of Jesus was marked by humility and his disciples should also claim that distinctive. Don't begin by challenging your professor in the classroom. Try to see him privately in his office, preferably during office hours. Don't enter his office loaded down with books and arguments with which to slay your Goliath. Remember—you may have misunderstood him. Ask him to explain those points again. (Most professors would be flattered to realize that the students cared enough about the lectures to desire clarification.) If it turns out 95 that he was, in fact, attacking the gospel, then explain to him why you are disturbed by his interpretation. He will be encouraged to share himself as a person with you if you initiate a personal approach.

It would be wise to ask him how he views students who differ with his interpretation of Christianity. Does he expect them to remain silent during his lectures or does he prefer interaction? But note that his actions may differ from his words. More than one student has had his grade reduced by a professor who "preferred interaction" as long as the prof would emerge the victor. If the professor demands that his students conform to the professorial party line on examinations, then the dissenting student may preserve his integrity by prefacing his answer with the statement, "According to our professor . . ." or, "The position presented in class stated. . . ." A student who has been given the freedom to express his own convictions in an exam should remember that a personal testimony is no substitute for adequate course preparation.

classroom duels usually fail

Should a student ever take issue with a professor in class? In most cases the answer would be negative. (A majority of my Christian colleagues answered that question "Never.") The professor has too many points of leverage over the average dissenter in class: he knows the subject better than you do, he has probably heard your objection on a number of previous occasions whereas this is your first time to stammer it out and he is much more accomplished in addressing a group. After all, it's his job. Besides, we professors are a rather sensitive and touchy crew with thin skins. I have heard more than one of my colleagues declare, "When a student takes issue with me in class, he forces me to slap him down." Beware of the teacher whose ego has been threatened. Another disadvantage to classroom confrontation is that you may lose the argument. You then run the risk of encouraging your fellow students to believe that Christianity has been discredited.

be honest as well as polite

In spite of these reservations you may conclude that God wants you to speak out in class. There are a number of ways to soften the confrontation. For instance, you may raise the question "Is this the only way in which scholars have answered this question?" or "Is this the only solution to this question that a thinking man can accept?" Any academician worth his salt will think twice before answering either question in the affirmative. One may also reduce ego involvement by using the preface "Some scholars have argued . . ." and then asking your instructor how he would respond to it. But don't be startled if he responds with data that you have never before encountered. Yet God does work through the foolish things of this world to confound the wise (1 Corinthians 1:20-30).

But what about a required course taught by a militant anti-Christian who uses his class as a platform from which he may attack Christianity? (This appears to happen most often in philosophy and in religion courses.) A helpful approach is for a number of Christian students to coordinate their schedules so that all of them will be taking the course simultaneously from the same professor. This would put them in a position to support each other by praying and discussing the issues together. It may even be possible for this group of Christian students to meet together with a Christian professor who could help them work through the difficult issues. This would be in keeping with the biblical emphasis upon the Christian community and would avoid the sad spectacle of the individual Christian venturing forth under his own strength. If the group is stymied by a tough question, it may be possible for them to write a Christian authority in the field. Christian scholars are always pressed for time but many would make the time to answer the inquiry.

There may be some cases in which it would be necessary to deal with a vehement anti-Christian through the administration. No college is interested in paying a faculty member just to spout off personal prejudices in class. Few students realize how vulnerable faculty are to the administration, especially during a period in which the number of qualified professors exceeds the available teaching posts. But this approach should be used very cautiously and only after prolonged prayer and consultation with older Christians. The method should be for a group of Christians, or representatives from campus religious organizations, to approach the appropriate administrative officer with their complaint in writing. There would be no need to request the dismissal of the professor. It is enough that students ask for a greater degree of academic freedom by having another of different persuasion also teach a section of the same course. In an era of student unrest most administrations would be glad to heed legitimate student grievances. It would provide the administration with an opportunity to demonstrate it is responsive to student needs. (If this strikes you as Machiavellian, remember that Paul claimed the rights of a Roman citizen in order that the gospel might be proclaimed.)

A final option open to Christians would be to schedule a series of public lectures or debates by outstanding Christian scholars who would address themselves to the critical questions being directed against the gospel on that particular campus. In some cases the lecture topics could be coordinated with the syllabus of an important required course such as Western civilization or philosophy. If the scholars were top-notch and if the Christians did a good job of publicizing the lectures, the 99 meetings could be flooded with non-Christian students.

It is difficult for a Christian to know what to do when his faith is under attack in class. We are told to "be prepared to make a defense to any one who calls you to account for the hope that is in you," yet it should be done "with gentleness and reverence" (1 Peter 3:15). It is only through the wisdom of God that the Christian student can discover the reality of what it means to be as wise as a serpent but as gentle as a dove.

MALE AND
FEMALE IN COMMUNITY

People want to learn what it means to live together in community. Communes are the most obvious evidence of this. The commune members emphasize sharing with each other everything from personalities to possessions. In Christian circles there is a growing consciousness of the need for "body life," a turning away from strong individualism and doctrinal schism to interdependence among Christian brothers and sisters.

Many Christian students are concerned to see community become a part of their lifestyle and are working toward that end. But 101 most of them are striving for community in an almost *asexual* sense: They do not appear to be aware of how their sexuality, their being male and female, enters into the building of or hindrance to community.

In many church circles a young person's entire education on sexuality is limited to one principle, "Thou shalt not have premarital sex." I whole-heartedly agree with that teaching, but I've also learned that sexuality is far more complex than just premarital sex. Sexuality shapes our lives. When I interact with another girl or with a man, young or old, I do so as a creature of sexuality.

Whenever any group is striving to build community, four kinds of interaction takes place: female to female, female to male, male to female, and male to male.

Let's begin with the female to female interaction and look at some of the barriers women have with each other, barriers that hinder the building of community.

female — female

When women interact, some characteristic attitudes are displayed. One of these attitudes is that during our college and young adult years girls don't need girl friends. These are the years we are to spend our prime time and energy almost exclusively in the building of male-female relationships.

Women are also prone to stereotyping each other. The next time you're in a room with a co-ed group, watch what happens when a new girl enters. The men, of course, look her over to see what kind of a "chick" she is. And the girls will also look her over, determine what type of female competitor she is and then, largely on that evaluation alone, will choose their mode of relating to her.

Women also covet each other's beauty and talents. This means, on one hand, that we basically reject or dislike the person God has made us to be. It also means that we look on other women with a jealously comparative eye. Am I exaggerating? Ask yourself how often you've heard one woman say to another, "I'm glad you're pretty," or "I'm glad you're so talented."

We females are constantly competing with each other for male attention. This makes us keep an affectional distance between us (it's hard to compete with someone you care about deeply). It also involves a cutthroat attitude of "my happiness first, at all costs."

These attitudes are not without their results. As women we are known for our cattiness (ask any man), loneliness and insecurity. You cannot compete with or ignore so large a portion of your world without suffering these effects.

Perhaps the most ironic result of these attitudes is that they undermine our relationships with men. Having learned to be superficial with women, we carry this over and remain superficial with men. Our insecurity brings out possessiveness: and if there's any trait that a man cannot tolerate in a woman it is possessiveness.

male — female

A second area which raises barriers to community is male to female interaction. The most common complaint I hear from girls is that they find it hard to respect the men they work or live with. Many times respect is faked.

I see three possible reasons for this. First, many men in our society base their manhood on false, external things—the car they drive, the "chicness" of their girlfriend, the income they have. These are supposed to equal masculinity. But the biblical view, especially as seen in Proverbs and the Gospels' view of Christ the man, is that masculinity is determined by a man's inner character. Would that men attempted to outdo each other in integrity, compassion and honesty as often as they do in sports.

Second, we women are becoming increasingly conscious that men do not always take us seriously as persons. They will deride a girl with many talents and gifts or they will demand that a girl "keep her place." Men give strong evidence of believing that because a woman is different from them she is, by that very fact, inferior. Have you ever made the statement, "Women are impossible to understand"? Perhaps you were really saying,

"Women are not important enough for me to take time to understand them. They should understand me, of course, because that's part of their role."

Third, it is a well-documented fact that men exploit women sexually. Perhaps the most irritating aspect of this exploitation is the flagrant double standard which operates on a man's behalf in society's laws and mores. A prime ingredient I seek in male-female relationships is trust—and exploitation utterly destroys trust.

female — male

Along similar lines, there are barriers to community in the way females relate to males. Experience and literature teach us that women have been given a certain degree of "woman power." We have the capacity to build up or tear down a man. Some women are conscious of this power and choose to use it wrongly. But the vast majority of girls are unconscious of their woman power. Out of ignorance they often misuse it.

How? I've learned from men that women exploit them sexually, just as they exploit us. We exploit them by our dress and our actions. We wear see-through blouses, tight pants and short skirts, and then wonder why men see us only as bodies. We play constant flirt games and then wonder why we are not shown more respect. I've heard a great many sermons on Matthew 5:28 soundly chastizing the men on 105 the subject of lust. Unfortunately, I've not yet heard any good sermon on Proverbs, which makes it very clear that one knows a harlot by her manner and her dress.

Women exploit men socially as well. They use men to gain status and fill their evenings. When a man risks himself and asks a girl for a date, he assumes her acceptance means she wants to get to know him. When he finds out she is "killing time," his personhood is insulted. This happened to one of my friends at the U. of Washington several times. He finally gave up dating for a period because he did not feel he could trust girls and didn't want to risk being used again.

In many groups, however, the greatest misuse of woman power is in the area of leadership. Most women expect and sincerely want the men to take the leadership, but they do not accept the responsibility to help men *learn* to be leaders. Whenever I hear girls in an Inter-Varsity chapter lamenting the lack of men, I begin asking questions: Do you give the men you have positive feedback or do you only complain? When there's a job to be done are you willing to take a chance on a younger brother or would you rather do it yourself? When a man makes an error do you let him quit or do you encourage him to try again? Do you make it known that your chapter needs male help or do you expect the word to spread by osmosis? In other words, are you taking positive, concrete action?

male — male

Finally, there are barriers to community growing out of males relating to males. Because of our societal stereotype of what constitutes masculinity, men seldom are open with each other regarding their feelings of fear, anxiety or inadequacy. This easily leads to game playing and superficiality.

Likewise, men do not comfortably know how to tell each other, "I love you." It is generally assumed that the respected person knows he is respected. But I know of at least one Inter-Varsity staff man who almost quit his work because of the lack of positive feedback. Students told others how much they respected him, but they never told him. This omission severely limits a man's ability to fulfill his God-given responsibility to "build up" the other person.

handling the barriers

One of the best things about being a Christian is that you are never left with only the problem. The Lord has given us a two-fold solution to our problems in community: the Spirit and the Word.

As Christians we can know the confidence that we have not been given "the spirit of fear; but [the Spirit] of power, and of love, and of a sound mind." When we work to build community we have the Spirit of "fellowship" to lead us.

We have the Old and New Testaments to

instruct us practically as a "household of faith." A few of these instructions include:

1. Looking honestly at ourselves to see if these barriers exist in our individual and corporate lives. We can then ask God for forgiveness and expect a change (Psalm 51:10; 1 John 1:9).

2. Reading, studying and talking with each other so that we can better understand our own sexuality and others' (Proverbs 4:7; Matthew 10:16). A recently-married friend made the observation that she was sorry she had waited until marriage to read and talk about sexuality. She realized that she could have been a better sister if she had understood herself and others before.

3. Learning how to "bear each other's burdens" (Galatians 6:2). This can mean many things: women accepting how men are built sexually and dressing respectfully, not exploitatively; or men looking into the truth in Women's Lib instead of just reacting against it and branding it all "lies and exaggerations."

4. Learning to "rejoice with those who rejoice" (Romans 12:15). For women this might mean being glad with the girl down the hall about her big date Friday night, even though you are staying home and watching television.

5. Thanking God for sexuality and for the richness it adds to community.

THE TRUTH ABOUT SEX

We pride ourselves on our ability to face the facts of life. We admire the capacity to look cool-eyed at reality, and this is especially true with regard to sex.

The irony of it all is that the kind of sex that has saturated our culture is a caricature of the real thing. The four-letter words which pockmark our literature, movies, conversation, and even our thought do not represent sex at all; they are expressions of eroticism which J. B. Priestley says is "the twanging of a single nerve—to the exclusion of everything else."

Christians, contrary to most contemporary opinion, are the people who know the truth about sex. They have learned this truth because they have faced the prior question of the truth about God, and about themselves. Having found God as Creator and Father through Jesus Christ, they are delivered from the negative atheism or the neutral agnosticism in which sex becomes so terribly confused. Having known God they have also found themselves, not as cosmic accidents or thinking animals, but as children of God in whom even sex has a purpose.

Christians know that sex is good and beautiful, not some mistake of evolution or goof of God. They revel in the knowledge, revealed in the first chapters of Genesis, that God deliberately built sexuality into his creatures. They see real beauty in the words, "It is not good that man should be alone," and in the knowledge that God created male and female, saying to them, "Be fruitful and multiply." They avoid the two mistakes made by moderns regarding sex: the puritanism which denies it and the paganism which worships it. Because they accept themselves as children of God, in Christ who was the Word made *flesh,* they are neither embarrassed by sex nor preoccupied with it. They are grateful for it without making it a god, they respect it without fearing it, and they see beauty in it without feeling guilty.

Christians know that sex is physical, but

not merely physical. They find the key to this insight in the words, "Therefore a man leaves his father and his mother and cleaves to his wife, and they become one flesh. And the man and his wife were both naked, and were not ashamed" (Genesis 2:24, 25). These beautiful words accept the reality of sexuality, but they also reveal the spiritual dimension of sex.

Sex, in its fulness, is the union of two people, not just two bodies. Almost universally sex is thought of in modern terms as exclusively physical. It is this superficial, distorted understanding of sex which has dominated modern thought and which is being "overemphasized." Sex, as God intended it, is the interpenetration of two personalities, not just two bodies. Christians know that sex without love is not sex at all. Many who have had extensive and sordid experience exploring and exploiting physical pleasures are almost totally ignorant of the truth about sex.

Thornton Wilder, in *The Bridge of San Luis Rey,* says: "Many who have spent a lifetime in it can tell us less of love than the child that lost a dog yesterday." The passionate grappling of two sweaty bodies does not in itself bring understanding or communication or fulfilment. In fact, it can leave both parties more isolated and desolate than ever if love is not involved as God intended. It is this lack of the spiritual dimension in sex which creates a narcotic need for more "kicks" resulting in the sadism and perversion which is called sex in our modern world.

But Christians also know that the kind of love that reveals the truth about sex is love that is total commitment. The new morality makes love the only worthy motive of human conduct, and so it is. However, when the passions are involved there is a high rise in the incidence of self-delusion. Any love that falls short of the total commitment of marriage is a love too weak to reveal the full power and glory of the truth about sex. Whenever the back door is left open so that two people may escape from their commitment to each other —as is always the case in premarital or extra-marital intercourse—a deep dimension of the sexual act always eludes them. There is an intercourse of personalities—of minds, and emotions and purposes and destinies—when two people are committed to each other in marriage which is never known in extra-marital affairs. It is no accident that the Hebrew verb "to know" is used repeatedly in the Old Testament to refer both to sexual intercourse and to the knowledge of God. Both require commitment. Polytheism and polygamy are not only degrading and destructive to human personality, they are alike in that they result in ignorance of God and of the truth about sex.

A few years ago I conducted the funeral service for a lady who had died of a wasting disease after a long illness. She and her husband had lived together for more than fifty years. After the funeral her husband, an old friend, wanted to talk. He described how his wife had called him into her room a few days before she died and had looked up at him from the bed and said simply, "Jim, I love you." These two had known the ecstasy of physical union, time and time again. They had known the joy of parenthood. Their bodies and their souls had had intercourse until they had blended into one. Total commitment, faithfulness and loyalty had revealed to them the truth about sex.

There is a great deal more to the facts of life than modern man knows. He will never learn about God until he commits himself, through Jesus Christ. He will never learn about sex until he commits himself in marriage.

THE REAL
STORY BEHIND THE FIFTH

17 Do you have trouble with your parents? If you do, don't write off the help God offers you. Look at Exodus 20:12. "Honor your father and mother, that your days may be long in the land which the Lord your God gives you."

Sound old-fashioned? Irrelevant? Like the same old worn-out advice? I don't think so. Stop and take a closer look at what God is *really* saying here.

First, this commandment is not directed toward small children. It is directed toward adults, or rather toward children who have grown up.

In the society to which this commandment was given, the father was king. His word was law, there was no higher court of appeal. He could be arbitrary, selfish, or perverse; he could even sell his family into slavery to pay off a debt.

But once a man married and left his father and mother, his relationship to them changed completely. Now he was king and they, all too often, were forgotten and abandoned. When the aged could no longer pull their own weight economically, they were cast out of society to die by exposure or to be killed by wild beasts. This was the societal norm.

But then came the commandment: Honor your parents when they have long since lost their financial usefulness. And civilization took a mighty leap forward.

So the fifth commandment is not something that we grow out of, but something we grow into. It is a responsibility we can assume only when we are no longer under obligation to our parents. It is assumed voluntarily, it is not demanded of us.

honor and obedience

Second, the commandment doesn't talk about obedience, it talks about honor. Anybody who thinks that honor and obedience are the same either has no backbone or knows nothing of conscience. The apostle Peter who wrote, "Honor the emperor" also said, "We ought rather to obey God than men." You 115 can honor those you disobey for conscience's sake. And you can dishonor those you obey. We are called to honor, not necessarily to obey.

A little child should, of course, obey his parents. If he doesn't, he's punished. This has little to do with honoring his parents. Perhaps only as the child outgrows the requirements of obedience can he have the opportunity of honoring.

To "honor," according to the Random House Dictionary, is to "regard with high public esteem." Parents who quote the fifth commandment to their children in an effort to get them to knuckle under to their demands have missed the point entirely. They may be able to create a disrespectful subservience, but that's the opposite of the commandment. Honoring is something I do freely, because I want to. It can't be demanded of me. It is something I do publicly and joyfully, not something I do shamefully while gritting my teeth. Honoring my parents means that I delight in them and acknowledge them with respect as people to whom I'm indebted more deeply than I could ever repay.

disobeying your parents

Third, some of the things our parents may desire or demand of us we must not do. So long as we live in their house, we're to abide by their rules. But we're not to abide by our parents' aspirations or expectations for us.

We're to become ourselves. In this we are responsible not to our parents, but to God. If our parents' intentions for us conflict with what we believe to be God's will, the difference in our loyalties should be as great as love and hate. Some of Jesus' harshest words were that no man can be His disciple unless he's willing to hate his mother and his father (Luke 14:26).

While in high school, I planned to follow in my father's footsteps. I'd won a four-year scholarship to the U. of Maryland to study electrical engineering and become a fire insurance executive. But I came to believe that God was calling me to enter the ministry instead. This completely contradicted my father's expectations for me. He couldn't understand why I was going to waste my life. He thought it was fanatical. But I had to refuse his expectations. It caused tremendous tension in my family which took about six years to heal. Recently my father has been struggling with multiple sclerosis and has begun to consider God more seriously. He now believes that God was trying to speak to him when I first became a Christian and took that stand. He feels that his rejection of God determined his harsh dealings with me at the time. And he's grateful that I refused to obey him and follow his expectations.

Having said all that, I find it interesting that this is the only one of the ten commandments that is stated positively. All the others are "thou shalt nots," but this one is a "thou shalt." It suggests to me that I'm being called upon to go beyond the normal, everyday requirements of righteousness. Perhaps in the moment I feel I must disagree with my parents, I'm to honor them most deeply.

think of the future

Fourth, this is the only one of the ten commandments with a promise attached to it. "Honor your father and your mother that your days may be long. . . ." There isn't anything magical about that. It is a piece of straightforward practical advice. A parable tells about a little old man who lived with his married son and daughter-in-law. His hands trembled, he had trouble eating, and he usually spilled things. So they made him a little table out in back. One day the couple noticed their own son playing with some bits of wood. They asked what he was doing, and he said, "I'm making a little table where I can feed you when I get big."

If you would like one day to be the sort of parent whose children find him honorable, you should begin today by being the sort of child who honors his parents.

CONCENTRATE ON EVERYTHING

18 John Wesley once stated that the devil hated the merger of piety and learning more than anything else. Finding this merger has been the continuing problem of my Christian life. I know what it means to have piety and zeal without the balance of knowledge.

During the summer between by sophomore and junior years of college, I smashed my thumb at work and had to have the thumb nail removed. After work in the evenings, I used to walk around the neighborhood to get my mind off the pain. One night I wandered into the back of a tent meeting because I thought it would be good entertainment. Following the meeting a boy about my age who had found Christ two years earlier caught up with me and began to talk to me about my relationship with God. Three days later on Sunday afternoon in my own home I felt stirred to read the Bible a girlfriend had given to me. In Matthew 3 I read the words of the voice that came out of heaven when Jesus was baptized: "This is my beloved Son, with whom I am well pleased." I thought, Can this be true? If Jesus is the Son of God from heaven, then this has to be the most startling discovery that any man could ever make. If it were true, all of life had to be different. Could I believe it? I had to decide. It was painful for me, but I chose to accept these words as true, and my life changed that Sunday afternoon.

I was profoundly impressed with three things which now control the emphases in my life. First, the providence of God, even in smashed thumbs! Second, the power and life of the Word of God to draw to Christ. Third, the importance of apologetics for removing prejudices about the Bible. I had resisted reading the Gospels because I thought they were all written hundreds of years after the first century. This young man simply showed me the dates of the books in his Bible. This was enough proof for me to at least listen to the Gospels. Without his help, I might have waited years to hear the gospel.

culture shock

After my conversion, I had a strong reaction to the whole cultural world around me because it seemed so alien to this new life I had found. I also reacted strongly to my college education because it had not led me to this reality. So I opted to drop out of college and join a fanatical group. I wrongly chose to substitute piety for learning. The devil won this time.

But God had another plan. As I was eligible for draft, I decided to enlist in the Air Force instead and pursue the electronics field. During the years I was stationed in Biloxi, Mississippi, I met a group of Christians who helped me get a more solid orientation in the Bible. I saw in these people a deep love for and devotion to Jesus Christ coupled with a profound knowledge of Scripture and God's world. I wondered if a person who knew so much could still be zealous for Jesus Christ.

When I finished my duty in the Air Force, I decided to complete my last year of college at Bryan College in Tennessee. That year at Bryan was the first time I spent in a Christian atmosphere. It was a great experience. I began to discover that I could immerse myself in studies and still walk with Jesus Christ.

From Bryan I went on to Dallas Seminary in Texas. There I found outstanding scholars who also deeply loved Jesus Christ and were firmly committed to the authority of Scripture over every area of life. Again, I found people who could combine authentic piety with thorough scholarship without compromising either.

But a problem developed in my life in seminary days. I found that I could bury myself in studies and eliminate any significant pursuit of God's presence in my life. My learning was crowding out my affection for Christ. I was tempted to give up the studies and the devil was about to win out again. But I realized that that would lead me right back to my earlier experience.

church history and heresy

So I wrestled with this problem of piety and learning. I began to notice how in the history of the church the emphasis on one extreme or the other always produced some sort of heresy. For example, an overemphasis on Aquinas' natural theology produced rationalism on the one hand and a counter-reaction of extreme subjectivism or irrationalism on the other. In the individual life pietism without the opposite extreme of learning quickly degenerates into fanaticism and excessive mysticism. Some of you are going through this right now. On the other hand an overemphasis on learning and reason without the cultivation of a personal relationship with God easily becomes a cold, reduced and non-reproductive form of Christianity.

The resolution of this problem for me came in recognizing that the truth lies in affirming both extremes at the same time. This is a paradox beautifully worked out in Virginia Mollenkott's book, *In Search of Balance* (Word, 1969).

We need a pursuit of God deep enough to make us thoroughly intellectual and an intellectual pursuit serious enough to make us zealous for the experience of God. The balance comes by including the two poles with equal passion in a balanced tension. Paul taught in Colossians that Jesus Christ is both Lord of redemption and Lord of all creation. We cannot afford to cycle from one extreme to the other or compromise at the center with lukewarmness.

These two poles are held in balance in a Christian community by a proper recognition of the gifts of the Holy Spirit. Some of us will be led by the Spirit of God to emphasize one or the other of these realities. But we will include both, if not with equal time at least with equal interest. The variety of individuals under the Holy Spirit moves the community toward the balance it needs.

I have found another problem. As I try to emphasize both the pursuit of God's presence and the pursuit of knowledge of his world, I tend to let my experience with Christ make me feel more spiritual than others. It breeds self-righteousness because I forget the depth of sin (which still touches my life) and the mystery of faith (you cannot program it through a formula). Then, too, I find that

there can be a quest for knowledge that
makes me feel superior to others. So I am
plagued with the ugly twin heads—the pride
of spirituality and the pride of intellectualism.
Both isolate me from others. I can develop an
individual piety that does not lead me to be
concerned for other people. I can follow the
pursuit of knowledge that makes me an island
unto myself instead of building bridges to
serve others.

judgment and instruction

I found Paul's words both judging and instruc-
ting me when he said, "You should be free to
serve each other in love" (Galatians 5:13,
Phillips). The further balance I needed was
found in Romans 12. Instead of striving to
exceed others in either piety or learning I was
to make it my aim to outdo the other person
in showing authentic love. My piety and learning were to be unto God alone, not unto
others. You can't serve others in love without
humbling yourself. And humility destroys
that pride which kills our interpersonal rela-
tions.

Yet even all this can become ingrown, pro-
vincial and self-centered. Soon the provisions
with which God has equipped us for service to
the world become tasteless and unattractive.
We begin to turn to more stimulating things
to fill the boredom. Have you ever had a picnic spoiled by rain and ended up eating the
picnic at home? Somehow it isn't appetizing

because it was designed for the other use. God's Word and our love for one another are designed by God to equip us for mission to the world that does not know the Father. If we are not mission oriented, we are not balanced.

Consider the apostle Paul as an example of these three sides of the Christian life. First, I see him as a Renaissance man—a man of encyclopedic interest, a man of books. He said to his friend as he wrote from the cold, damp and dim Mamertine prison in Rome, "Timothy, when you come don't forget the books and especially the parchments" (2 Timothy 4:13). But Paul balanced this with a view of the lordship of Christ mediated through the Scriptures, "[We] take every thought captive to obey Christ" (2 Corinthians 10:5). This suggests that he was a Reformation man even though he lived before the Reformation was born. Yet he was more than a man of books, and a man of the Book, he was a man of mission in his life also. "I endure everything for the sake of the elect, that they also may obtain the salvation which in Christ Jesus goes with eternal glory" (2 Timothy 2:10). These three images record the balanced life of a man whose fruitfulness for God was immense.

If the devil hates the wedding of piety and learning more than anything else it may be that the thing God delights in most is their balanced expression in our Christian life and mission.